SO-BZW-717

Indonesia
phrasebook

Margit Meinhold

Indonesia Phrasebook

Published by
Lonely Planet Publications
PO Box 88, South Yarra
Victoria 3141, Australia

Printed by
Colorcraft, Hong Kong

Design & Illustrations by
Graham Imeson

Typesetting by
Ann Logan

First published
June 1984 (with corrections May 1986)

National Library of Australia
Cataloguing in Publication Data

Meinhold, Margit.
Indonesia phrasebook.

ISBN 0 908086 55 5.

1. Indonesia language – Conversation and
phrase books – English. I. Title.

499'.22183'421

Copyright © Lonely Planet, 1984

All rights reserved. No part of this publication may be reproduced, stored
in a retrieval system or transmitted in any form by any means, electronic,
mechanical, photocopying, recording or otherwise, except brief extracts
for the purpose of review, without the written permission of the publisher
and copyright owner.

Contents

Contents

SCRIPT

A note on script. Indonesian is written using Roman letters. This is an adaptation from an earlier Arabic derivation. The words are phonetically spelt, using a system which was updated in 1972. You are likely to see signs in all three variations: Arabic; Roman before 1972; and Roman after 1972, when the early spelling was standardised. The four changes are:

tj – c	j – y
dj – j	ch – kh

Pronunciation

Indonesian is a very easy language to learn, and even easier to pronounce. Each single letter represents a sound. The sounds are the same every time and receive equal emphasis. Generally the last syllable in a word is stressed. In sentences, stress the most important word.

Pronunciation is consistently the same for each letter, with one or two exceptions. Most sounds are the same as English sounds but here is a list of pronunciations of vowel and consonant sounds where confusion may arise.

Vowels

a is pronounced like the **u** in 'hut' or 'up'.

Apa kabar?	How are you?
Kabar baik.	Fine thanks.

e is a short sound, like the **e** in 'bet', but it is not always pronounced. For example, the greeting *selamat*, is pronounced **slamat**. An **e** at the end of a word is a little longer.

Selamat sore	'slamat soray'	Good afternoon

i is pronounced like the **i** sound in 'unique'. The length of the sound doesn't alter.

Selamat tidur	'slamat tidur'	Good night
Selamat tinggal	'slamat ting garl'	Farewell (said when leaving)

o is similar to the English sound in either 'hot' or 'cold'. Generally speaking you won't be misunderstood if you pronounce this sound as you would in English.

foto	photograph	
oto	car	

u is pronounced like the 'oo' in 'too', only shorter.

satu	'satoo'	one
dua	'doo a'	two

There are also three vowel combinations: **ai**, **au** and **ua**. The sounds of the individual vowels do not change, they are simply run on by sliding from one to the other.

ai sounds like 'i' in 'line'

Kabar baik	'kabar bike'	I'm fine.

au sounds like a drawn out 'ow' like 'cow'.

Saudara	'sowdara'	You or brother
mau	'mow'	want

ua at the start of a word is rather like a 'w' sound.

uang	'wang'	money

Consonants

The pronunciation of consonants is very straightforward. Each is pronounced consistently and most sound like English consonants.

c is always pronounced ch' as in 'chair'.

karcis	'karchis'	ticket

g is always pronounced hard, as 'g' in 'garden'.

pagi	'pagi'	morning
tinggal	'ting gal'	life

ng at the end of a word is always pronounced like 'ng' at the end of 'sing'.

siang	'siang'	day (11 am to 3 pm)

j is pronounced as 'dj'. It's the sound you hear at the beginning of 'join'.

tujuh	'tudjuh'	seven

r is pronounced very clearly and distinctly. It is always slightly trilled.

Apa kabar	'apa kabarrr'	How are you?
Selamat tidur	'slamat tidurrr'	good night

h is always pronounced, except at the end of a word. It is stressed a little more strongly than in English, as if you were sighing. This heavy pronunciation is particularly true for words of Arabic origin, when the 'h' appears between two vowels which are the same.

hotel	'hhotel'	hotel
mahal	'mahhhal'	expensive
rupiah	'rupia'	local currency

k is pronounced the same as the English 'k', except when it appears at the end of a word. Here you should stop just short of actually saying the 'k'.

Kabar baik	'kabar bai'	I'm well.

ny is a single sound like the beginning of 'new', before the 'oo' part of the word.

    nyonya   'nyonya'   Mrs.

Grammar

Indonesian grammar is simple to master for the purpose of basic communication. Nouns do not have plural forms. The pattern of the sentence is generally: subject, verb, object. Sentences are usually short.

VERBS

Indonesian has a basic verb form which may be used in colloquial speech. You will be understood perfectly well when you use this basic form.

Verbs do not change their form for tense. Terms for time, like *besok* (tomorrow), and *kemarin* (yesterday), can be put at the beginning of sentences to show tense.

There is a system of adding suffixes and prefixes to some verbs. This is extremely complicated and need not be mastered here.

ADJECTIVES

There are no articles like 'a' or 'the' to worry about. Nouns come first, and anything about them succeeds them.

this book	*buku itu*
my book	*buku saya*
red book	*buku merah*

When you want to say more than one thing about the noun you use ... *yang* ...

the small red book	*buku merah yang kecil*

Comparisons in Indonesian are very similar to English comparisons. The comparative form precedes the adjective..

more	*lebih*
most	*paling*
the bigger hotel	*hotel lebih besar.*
the biggest shop	*toko paling besar.*

SENTENCES

The word order for Indonesian sentences is the same as for English sentences: subject, verb, object. There are no special terms for 'is' and 'are'.

Buku merah, on its own, means 'The book is red'.

For sentences where no subject is obvious the word *ada* is used. *Ada* may mean 'there is', 'there are', so that:

Ada buku merah, for example, means 'There is a red book'.

This term is the nearest eqivalent to 'is', but means 'to be' in the sense of 'to exist'. It may also be used to indicate possession, or for emphasis.

TENSE

Tense is indicated by context, not by inflection. This means that you may place a time word, like 'tomorrow' or 'yesterday', in front of the sentence. For a list of time words, see the section on numbers. Alternatively you may use a verb like *mau*.

    Mau means want, but can also mean will or shall. The verb *akan* means wish or will, as does *hendak*.

To illustrate sentence construction better, here are a few verbs:

to eat	*makan*
to drink	*minum*
to want	*mau*
to go	*pergi*

The man eats chicken. *Orang itu makan ayam.*
The children go to the shop. *Anak-anak pergi ke toko.*
I want to drink tea. *Saya mau minum teh.*
They want to sleep. *Mereka mau tidur.*

NEGATION

Tidak and *bukan* are used. Both mean 'not ' or 'no'. *Tidak* is put in front of verbs and adjectives, and *bukan* is put in front of nouns:

I do not want it. *Saya tidak mau.*
The book is not red. *Buku itu bukan merah.*
It is not a ticket. *Bukan karcis.*

Both words can be used on their own to mean 'No' in answer to a question.

QUESTIONS

The structure of question sentences is not difficult to master. You can make a question by simply raising the pitch of your voice at the end of the sentence.

There are a number of question words you may want to use as well. They are put at the beginning of the sentence.

what   *apa*   *Apa kabar?*
                             How are you? ('What news')

who	*siapa*	*Siapa nama?*
		What is your name. ('Whose name')
when	*kapan*	*Kapan bis pergi?*
		When does the bus go?
when	*bilamana*	*Bilamana ia tiba?*
		When did he arrive?
where	*dimana*	*Dimana stasiun?*
		Where is the station?
from where	*darimana*	*Darimana?*
		Where are you from?
to where	*kemana*	*Kemana bis pergi?*
		Where does the bus go to?
how/in what way	*bagaimana*	*Bagaimana kita makan?*
		How do we eat?
how much/ many	*berapa*	*Berapa harga ini?*
		How much is this?
why	*mengapa*	*Mengapa bis terlambat?*
		Why is the bus late?
may I	*boleh*	*Boleh saya makan ayam?*
		May I eat chicken?

A third possible way to make a question is by the addition of *-kah* to the end of the most important word, i.e. the word which the question is about. You may wish to make use of this when you have aquired a certain amount of proficiency. You can certainly get by without it.

Questions about you and your life will be asked quite frequently, in particular, *Sudah kawin?* 'Are you already married?' Unless you are indeed married, the appropriate answer is *Belum!*

already	*sudah*
not yet	*belum*
no	*tidak*

Note: *Tidak* would be grammatically fine to use, but most Indonesians would not understand why you should not be married or not thinking about it. You will get on a lot better, especially as a woman, if you answer *sudah* or *belum*.

PLURALS

The same word is used for singular or plural. There are no endings in Indonesian which may be attached to a word to make it plural. Generally the context will indicate whether something is plural or not. For example *banyak orang*, many people.

Occasionally a word is doubled.

| child | *anak* |
| children | *anak-anak* |

Doubling has several other functions. It can sometimes intensify the actual meaning of the word.

slow	*pelan*
slowly	*pelan-pelan*
road	*jalan*
walking	*jalan-jalan*

Because of this potential for confusion it's probably best to avoid indiscriminate doubling. Quantity can be indicated by a number, or a quantity word placed before the noun. Numbers are given in a chapter of the same name.

Quantity words

all	*semua*
both	*keduanya*
each	*tiap-tiap*
enough	*cukup*
every	*masing-masing*
little	*sedikit*
many/much	*banyak*
some	*beberapa, lain*

These words precede the noun they qualify.

There are many people.	*Banyak orang.*

OTHER USEFUL WORDS
Adverbs

always	*selalu*
also	*juga*
at once	*serentak*
between	*antara*
immediately	*dengan segara*
just	*baru*
never	*tak pernah*
often	*sering*
only	*hanya*
perhaps	*barangkali*
possibly	*mungkin*
rather	*agak*
really	*sungguh*
too	*terlalu*
very	*sekali*
yet	*toh*

Conjunctions

after	*sesudah*
as soon as	*segara*
before	*sebelum*
if	*kalau*
or	*atau*
since	*sejak*
when	*waktu*
while	*sedang*

Prepositions

about	*tentang*
at, in, on	*di*
because	*karena*
during	*selama*
for	*untuk*
from	*dari*
on, at	*pada*
since	*sejak*
through	*melalui*
till	*sampai*
to	*ke*
with	*dengan*
without	*tanpa*

PERSONAL PRONOUNS

I, my	*saya*
you	*kamu*
he, she	*ia* or *dia*
we	*kami* or *kita*
you	*saudara* or *kamu*
they	*mereka*

Personal pronouns reflect levels of politeness, so that *saudara* – you, (lit. brother) is the more formal version of *kamu* – you. *Kamu* is used only with friends. The second person plural (we) also has two versions: *kita* – we, including the person spoken to; and *kami*, which only includes the people spoken about and not the person being addressed.

POSSESSION

The personal pronouns are used to indicate possession. They are unchanged and placed after the noun. Nouns following nouns may also indicate possession.

my jacket	*jaket saya*
your ticket	*karcis saudara*
Mina's hotel	*hotel Mina*

Greetings & Civilities

In English we can say 'Good morning' or 'Good evening' or 'Good day', depending on the time of day. It's the same in Indonesian.

Good morning 7 am – 11 am	*Selamat pagi*
Good day 11 am – 3 pm	*Selamat siang*
Good afternoon 3 pm – 7 pm	*Selamat sore*
Good evening after dark	*Selamat malam*
Good night on retiring	*Selamat tidur*
Enjoy your meal	*Selamat makan*
Enjoy your drink	*Selamat minum*
Farewell on leaving	*Selamat tinggal*
Farewell on staying	*Selamat jalan*
Welcome	*Selamat datang*
See you later	*Sampai jumpa lagi*

Selamat comes from an Arabic word which means 'May your action be blessed'. Putting this word together with 'morning' or 'evening' then translates into something like 'Have a nice morning', etc. All sorts of actions may be blessed, and *selamat* is a word you will hear quite often.

Please/help	*Tolong*	*Tolong tutup pintu itu* Please shut the door
Please	*Silakan*	*Silakan masuk* Please come in
Thankyou	*Terima kasih*	
You're welcome	*Kembali*	
You're welcome (colloquial)	*Sama-sama*	
I'm sorry . . . (apology)	*Ma'af . . .*	*Ma'af, meja ini sudah dipesan.* I'm sorry but this table is reserved
Pardon? (What did you say)	*Ma'af?*	
Excuse me	*Permisi*	*Permisi, dimana ada hotel?* Excuse me, where is the hotel?

FORMS OF ADDRESS

In Indonesia you will hear two forms of address. The most usual is the *Bu/Pak* combination. These words literally mean Mother and Father. Consequently they may not be used in situations which require a greater show of respect or a greater degree of formality, like a passport office. In these situations you would be better advised to use the more formal *Tuan* and *Nyonya*. *Saudara* literally means brother or sister and when used when you want to say 'you', also shows a degree of respect. When talking to children you may want to use *kamu*.

Mr	*Bapak, Pak*
Mrs	*Ibu, Bu*
Mr. Sir	*Tuan*
Mrs. Madam	*Nyonya*
Miss	*Nona*

Small Talk

As you travel around Indonesia you may want to tell people about yourself. You will almost certainly be asked questions about yourself and the members of your family. These sentences may be turned into questions by raising your voice at the end.

My nationality is . . .	*Kebangsaan saya . . .*
Australian	*orang Australi*
American	*orang Amerika*
Canadian	*orang Kanada*
Danish	*orang Denmark*
Dutch	*orang Belanda*
English	*orang Ingerris*
French	*orang Perancis*
German	*orang Jerman*
foreigner	*orang asing*

My occupation is . . .	*Pekerjaan saya . . .*
artist	*seniman*
businessman	*pengusaha*
farmer	*petani*
sailor	*pelaut*
singer	*penyani*
teacher	*guru*
writer	*penulis*
nurse	*jururawat*
doctor	*dokter*

My religion is . . .	*Agama saya . . .*
Christian	*orang Nasrani*
Jewish	*orang Jahudi*
Muslim	*orang Islam*

Most Indonesians are Muslim, some are Buddhist, a few are Hindu. Throughout Indonesia there are also a few exotic religions, like Wektu Telu, which is unique to Lombok. If you are an atheist or an agnostic, it is not necessary to state this. You will maintain better relations by claiming to be a Christian, and even then it is likely that the children will feel sorry for you.

The Family — *Keluarga*

mother	*ibu*
father	*bapak*
brother, sister	*saudara*
older sister	*kakak*
older brother	*abang*
younger brother/sister	*adik*
child	*anak*
children	*anak-anak*
boy, son	*laki-laki*
girl, daughter	*perempuan*
husband	*suami*
wife	*isteri*

Some useful phrases

How are you?	*Apa kabar?*
I'm fine, thanks.	*Kabar baik.*
What's your name?	*Siapa nama anda?*

My name is . . .	*Nama saya . . .*
Are you married?	*Sudah kawin?*
Do you have chiildren?	*Sudah punya anak?*
Where do you come from?	*Darimana?*
Where are you going?	*Kemana?*
How old are you?	*Berapa umur?*
I don't understand.	*Saya tidak mengerti.*

Accommodation

Indonesian hotels range in price and standard from the low to the high end of the market. Hotels of the Hilton and Hyatt style are found in the larger tourist areas. Cheaper and more interesting are the *losmen* – Indonesian hotels – which are also more abundant. The standard of these *losmen* ranges from very traditional, simple hotels with basic rooms (four walls and a couple of beds) and an outside bathroom called a *mandi*, to rooms with showers and air-conditioning.

At the hotel

The hotel is near . . .	*Hotel dekat . . .*
the street.	*jalan*
the alley	*gang*
the beach	*pantai*
the shop	*toko*
Do you have . . .	*Adakah . . .*
a room	*kamar*
a bath	*mandi*
a toilet	*kamar kecil*
a bed	*meja*
a mirror	*cermin*
soap	*sabun*
towels	*handuk*
I will stay . . .	*Saya akan tinggal . . .*
one night	*satu malam*
two weeks	*dua minggu*
three months	*tiga bulan*

I want to eat . . .	*Saya mau makan . . .*
breakfast	*makan pagi*
lunch	*makan siang*
dinner	*makan malam*
I want to drink . . .	*Saya mau minum . . .*
tea	*teh*
coffee	*kopi*
hot water	*air panas*
cold water	*air dingin*
boiled water	*air putih*
How much is . . .	*Berapa sewa . . .*
the bill	*rekening*
the room a day	*kamar sehari*
for one person	*untuk se orang*
for breakfast	*untuk makan pagi*
for tax	*pajak*
service charge	*onkos pelayanan*

Some useful words

bathe	*mandi*
blanket	*selimut*
board (n)	*rumah kos*
candle	*lilin*
chair	*kursi*
clean (adj)	*bersih*
crowded	*ramai*
deposit	*titip*
dirty	*kotor*
door	*pintu*
dust (n)	*debu*
eat (v)	*makan*
electricity	*listrik*

garden	*kebun*
hedge	*pagar*
key, lock	*kunci*
pillow	*bantal*
servant	*pembantu*
sheet	*seperai*
noisy	*ramai*
quiet	*tenang*
rent (v)	*menyewa*
roof	*atap*
sit (v)	*duduk*
sleep (v)	*tidur*
table	*meja*
wake (v)	*bangun*
wash (v)	*cuci*

Some useful phrases

Do you have a room available?

Ada kamar kosong?

May I leave my passport with you?

Boleh saya titip paspor saya dengan tuan?

How long are you staying here?

Berapa lama anda akan tinggal disini?

Does the price include breakfast?

Apakah sewanya termasuk makan pagi?

Please spray my room. There are mosquitos in it.

Tolong menyemprot kamar saya. Ada nyamuk didalam.

I'm leaving this hotel. Please have my bill made up.

Saya akan meninggalkan losmen ini. Tolong disiapkan rekening saya.

Getting Around

Travelling in Indonesia is a slow business, so you don't want to be in a hurry. Departure times are usually approximate, although this is not always so. A lot of projects are underway to improve the condition of the roads but this work is done by hand and takes time so long distance travel on those bumpy roads can be *lekak-lekuk* – tedious and uncomfortable. Night buses are expresses and even day buses don't generally make stops at public conveniences. Buses and bemos are usually overcrowded so if it's at all possible organise yourself to sit in the middle, but not over the wheel, and avoid sitting next to the driver as the gear changes will ruin you kneecaps. If the price is not posted up somewhere, as it usually is for sea travel, you may bargain for a reduction of the fare. If the ticket counter is closed, the head of the bus station or boat office will help you.

Where can I catch a ...	*Dimana saya akan naik ...*
bus	*bis*
night bus	*bis malam*
train	*kereta api*
truck	*prahoto*
ship	*kapal*
boat	*prahu*
small boat	*sampan*
Where can I rent a ...	*Dimana bisa menyewa ...*
car	*mobil*
bicycle	*sepeda*
motor cycle	*sepeda motor*

What time does the bus ...	*Jam berapa bis ...*
depart	*berangkat*
stop	*berhenti*
arrive	*datang*
return	*kembali*

Directions

north	*utara*
south	*selatan*
east	*timur*
west	*barat*
left	*kiri*
right	*kanan*
in the middle	*ditengah*
at the front	*dimuka*
at the back	*belakang*

Some useful words

alley	*gang*
airport	*lapangan udara*
bus station	*stasiun, terminal bis*
cabin	*ruang*
corner	*sudut*
confirmation	*penegasan*
dock	*dok*
early	*pagi-pagi*
economy class	*kelas ekonomi*
emergency	*darurat*
empty (adj)	*koson*
fast	*cepat*
full	*ramai*

harbour	*pelabuan*
intersection	*persimpangan*
landing	*pendaratan*
late	*terlambat*
lounge	*kamar tunggu*
plane	*pesawat terbang*
port	*kiri kapal*
reservation	*pesenan tempat*
river	*sungai*
sail	*layar*
sea	*laut*
seat	*tempat duduk*
seat belt	*sabuk*
stationmaster	*kepala stasiun*
steward	*pramugara*
street	*jalan*
take off	*berangkat*
timetable	*daftar*
ticket	*karcis*
ticket window	*loket*

Some useful phrases

Where can I buy a bus ticket?
  Dimana saya bisa beli karcis bis?
Where is the ticket window?
  Dimana ada loket?
I'm lost.
  Saya tersesat.
Where is the nearest bus station?
  Dimana stasiun bis yang paling dekat?
Does this train go to . . . ?
  Apakah kereta api ini menuju ke . . . ?

Where do I get off to go to the bank?
Dimana saya turun jika pergi ke bank?
Excuse me, is this seat taken?
Permisi, apakah kursi ini kosong?
This seat is taken.
Kursi ini sudah ada orangnya.
Where are we now?
Dimana kita sekarang.

Around Town

This section has information about ordinary Indonesian towns, the names for the common features, etc, as well as separate sections on activities you may be involved in while in town, such as going to the post office, the bank or dealing with bureaucracy in general.

Where is the . . .	*Dimana ada . . .*
bank	*bank*
barong dance	*tatrian barong*
bookshop	*toko buku*
cinema	*bioskop*
concert	*konser*
How far is the . . .	*Berapa jauh . . .*
crossroad	*perempatan*
garden	*kebun*
hospital	*rumah sakit*
hotel	*hotel*
market	*pasar*
I am going to the . . .	*Saya pergi ke . . .*
museum	*musium*
park	*taman*
police	*polisi*
puppet theatre	*wayang kulit*
restaurant	*rumah makan*
school	*sekolah*
I want to see the . . .	*Saya mau lihat . . .*
temple	*kuil*
theatre	*gedung sandiwara*

town square	*alun-alun*
village	*desa*
zoo	*kebun binatang*

Some useful words

crowded	*ramai*
empty	*kosong*
expensive	*mahal*
interesting	*menarik hati*
nice	*bagus*
ticket	*karcis*

Some useful phrases

At what theatre can I see a play?
Di teater mana boleh saya menonton sandiwara?
How did you enjoy the play?
Sukakah anda pada sandiwara itu?
I am interested in music.
Saya suka seni musik.

At the post office

Where is the post office?	*Dimana ada kantor pos?*
I want to buy . . .	*Saya mau beli . . .*
postcards	*kartu pos*
stamps	*meterai pos*
I want to send a . . .	*Saya mau kirim . . .*
letter	*surat*
parcel	*paket*
telegram	*kawat*
Please send it . . .	*Silahkan . . .*
air mail	*pos udara*
surface mail	*pos biasa*

| express (overseas) | *ekspres* |
| express (internal) | *kilat* |

Some useful words

aerogramme	*aerogram*
envelope	*amplop*
extension (phone)	*sambungan*
long distance (phone)	*panggilan jauh*
operator	*operator*
phone booth	*sel*
phone number	*nomor telefon*
postage	*bea*
public phone	*telefon umum*
receiver (letter)	*penerima*
sender (letter)	*pengirim*
wrong number	*salah nomor*

Some useful phrases

I want to make a long distance call to Australia.
  Saya mau panggilan jauh ke Australia.
The line is busy.
  Telefonnya sedang bicara.
Sorry, you have the wrong number.
  Ma'af, anda salah nomor.
How much is an airmail letter to America?
  Berapa perankonya kirim surat dengan pos udara ke Amerika?
Please send this parcel to England by surface mail.
  Kirimkan paket ini ke England dengan pos biasa.
Please weigh this letter.
  Tolong timbang berat surat ini.

Please stamp this letter immediately.
Tolong tempelkan surat ini sekarang.

At the Bank

I want to change ...	*Saya mau menukar ...*
American dollars	*dolar Amerika*
Australian dollars	*dolar Australi*
bank draft	*surat wesel*
cash	*uang kontan*
cheque	*cek*
letter of credit	*surat kredit*
money	*uang*
travellers' cheque	*cek turis*

Some useful words

bank clerk	*pegawai bank*
bill, note	*uang kertas*
branch	*cabang*
commission	*komisi*
endorsement	*pengesyahan*
I.D. card	*K.T.P.*
signature	*tandatangan*
teller	*kasir*
ticket window	*loket*

Some useful phrases

What time does the bank open?
Jam berapa bank buka?
Where can I cash a travellers' cheque?
Dimana boleh saya menguangkan cek perjalanan turis?

What is the exchange rate?
> *Berapa perbandingan harga?*

Has any money arrived for me?
> *Ada pengirman untuk saya?*

Bureaucracy

If you need to have dealings with the Indonesian bureaucracy for any reason, there are a couple of things you ought to remember. Always dress decently. Try to speak to the person in charge; you will get more information this way and there is a good chance he/she will speak some English. With their English and your Indonesian you won't have many problems. In descending order of importance the official titles are:

head of province	*bupati*
head of a district	*camat*
head of an area	*kepala desa*
village chief	*kepala kampung*

Forms

name	*nama*
address	*alamat*
date of birth	*tanikh lahir*
place of birth	*tempat lahir*
age	*umur*
nationality	*kebangsaan*
religion	*agama*
identification	*surat keterangan*
passport number	*nomor paspot*
reason for travel	*maksud kunjungan*
profession	*pekerjaan*
marital status	*kawin*

Food

The simplicity of Indonesian is very easy to see when it comes to words connected with food and eating. *Makan* is both the verb 'to eat' and the noun 'food'. A restaurant is a 'house food' or *rumah makan*. Breakfast is 'morning food' or *makan pagi*. It couldn't be easier, could it?

Where is the ...	*Dimana ada ...*
restaurant	*rumah makan*
food stall	*warung*
night market	*pasar malam*

Please bring a ...	*Beri saya se ...*
menu	*daftar*
plate	*piring*
glass	*gelas*
knife and fork	*pisau dan garpu*
spoon	*sendok*
napkin	*serbet*
cup	*cangkir*

Meals

breakfast	*makan pagi*
lunch	*makan siang*
dinner	*makan malam*

Meat — *Daging*

beef	*daging sapi*
brains	*otak*

chicken	*ayam*
duck	*daging bebek*
heart	*jantung*
lamb	*domba*
liver	*hati*
mutton	*kambing*

Fruit *Buah*

apples	*apel*
banana	*pisang*
coconut	*kelapa*
durian	*durian*
lemon	*jeruk asam*
mangosteen	*manggis*
mango	*mangga*
orange	*jeruk manis*
papaya	*betik*
peanuts	*kacang*
pineapple	*nanas*
strawberry	*arbai*

Vegetables *Sayur*

cucumber	*mentimun*
beans	*buncis*
onion	*bawang*
potato	*kentang*

Most vegetables are simply called *sayur*, without having an individual name. If you are a vegetarian you can say *tanpa daging* – without meat, or *sayur saja* – vegetables only.

Staples

rice	*nasi*
noodles	*mie*
bread	*roti*

Snacks

cake	*kue*
biscuits	*biskit*
sweets	*gula-gula*
boiled egg	*telur rebus*
egg	*telur*

Spices

chilli	*lombok*
curry	*kari*
ginger	*jahe*
pepper	*merika*
salt	*garam*
soy sauce	*kecap asin*
sweet soy sauce	*kecap manis*
sugar	*gula*

Fish *Ikan*

salt water fish	*ikan laut*
fresh water fish	*ikan danau*
clams	*apitan*
lobster	*udang karang*
oysters	*tiram*

shrimp	*udang*
crab	*kepiting*

Drinks	*Minum*
beer	*bir*
boiled water	*air putih*
chocolate	*coklat*
citrus juice	*es jeruk*
coconut milk	*es kelapa*
coffee	*kopi*
cordial	*es stroop*
ginger tea	*jahe*
milk	*susu*
rice wine	*brem*
tea	*teh*

Some Prepared Food

nasi putih	plain white cooked rice
nasi goreng	fried rice, mainly rice
nasi sayur	rice and vegetables
nasi campur	rice with a selection of things including meat
mie kuah	noodle soup
sop ayam	chicken soup
cap cai	mixed vegetables (Chinese dish)
babi guling	roast piglet
gado-gado	cold vegetable salad with peanut sauce
sate	meat grilled on skewers
fu yong hai	omelette with meat and vegetables
martabak	pancake with accompaniments

Some useful words

bitter	*pahit*
boil (v)	*merebus*
cold	*dingin*
cook (v)	*masak*
delicious	*enak*
eat (v)	*makan*
foreign	*asing*
fresh	*baru*
fry (v)	*goreng*
hot	*panas*
indigenous	*asli*
good	*bagus*
salty	*asin*
slice (v)	*iris*
sour	*asam*
spicy	*pedas*
sweet	*manis*
no sugar	*tanpa gula*
unripe/uncooked	*mentah*

Some useful phrases

Can we have breakfast at this food stall?
Bagaimana jika kita makan pagi di warung ini?
I'm sorry but this table is reserved.
Ma'af, meja ini sudah dipesan.
We're in a hurry. Please bring our orders quickly.
Kami terburu-buru. Tolong cepatkan pesanan kami.
May we have our bill please?
Coba berikan rekening saya?

Shopping

It is customary to bargain in Indonesia, although prices can be set in some places, expecially when you are away from tourist oriented establishments. Fixed prices – *harga pas* – are often written onto the item or there may be a sign in the shop. It is quite common for tourists to be charged more than the local people. Tourists are wealthy! Even so, tourists do not usually pay a great deal more than the locals and if you want to know the common price – *harga biasa*, ask an independent bystander. On the public transport system watch what everybody else is paying. For long trips, or boat trips, expect to pay a little more than the locals. Bargaining is part of the way of life in Indonesia. If you treat it like a game it can be fun, even worthwhile, but remember that the 500 rupiah price difference you may be getting so upset about is really only about 50 cents to you.

Where is the ...	*Dimana ada ...*
market	*pasar*
night market	*pasar malam*
bookshop	*toko buku*
drug store	*toko obat*
tailor	*penjahit*
barber	*tukang pangkas*

I want to buy ...	*Saya mau beli ...*
that basket	*tas itu*
that bottle	*botol itu*
buttons	*kancing*
cigarettes	*rokok*
clothing	*pakain*
combs	*sisir*
film	*film*
hammer	*palu*
hat	*topi*
jar	*toples*
matches	*korek*
mosquito net	*kelambu*
rope	*tampar*
sandals	*sandel*
sarong material	*kain sarong*
shampoo	*keramas*
shoe laces	*tali spatu*
suitcase	*kopor*
swimsuit	*pakaian mandi*
tampons	*tampon*
thread	*benang*
toilet paper	*kertas kamar kecil*
toothbrush	*sikatgigi*
torch	*obor*
towel	*handuk*
underwear	*pakaian dalam*

Bookshop   *Toko Buku*

Give me . . .   *Beri . . .*

the morning newspaper	*koran pagi*
a magazine	*majalah*
a pocket dictionary	*kamus kantong*
a two-language dictionary	*kamus dua bahasa*
envelopes	*amplop*
writing paper	*kertas tulis*
ball point pen	*pena bolpoin*

Souvenir shopping

I would like . . .   *Saya akan suka . . .*

jewellery	*intan permata*
gold	*mas*
silver	*perak*
woodcarving	*ukiran kayu*
leather	*kulit*
bone	*tulang*
ivory	*gading*
material	*kain panjang*
printed batik	*batik cap*
stone	*batu*
puppets	*wayang kulit*
horn	*tanduk*
masks	*topeng*
hand-made batik	*batik tulis*
paintings	*lukisan*

Camera shop

camera	*alat pemotret*
black and white	*hitam/putih*

film	*film*
colour	*warna*
photograph	*foto*
to develop	*mencuci*

Colours

colour	*warna*
red	*merah*
yellow	*kuning*
black	*hitam*
blue	*biru*
green	*hijau*
brown	*coklat*
white	*putih*

Some useful words

big	*besar*
buy (v)	*beli*
cheap	*murah*
expensive	*mahal*
export (adj)	*mengekspor*
import (adj)	*impor*
insurance	*assuransi*
like (v)	*suka*
made in	*dibuat di*
old (adj)	*tua*
order (v)	*suruh*
parcel (n)	*bungkus*
prefer (v)	*lebih suka*
quality	*kwalitet*
quantity	*jumlah*
round	*bulat*

sell (v)	*jual*
small	*kecil*
style	*macam*
want(v)	*mau*

Some useful phrases

What is the normal price of this?
Berapa harga biasa itu?

May I try this on?
Boleh saya coba?

May I bargain?
Boleh saya tawar?

I'd like to look at blouses.
Saya ingin melihat-lihat blus.

How much is this?
Berapa harga ini?

Where are these goods made?
Barang-barang ini dibuat dimana?

Do I need insurance?
Apakah saya perlu asuransi?

free of charge
percuma

Where is the camera shop?
Dimana ada toko pemotret?

Please develop this film.
Bisa mencuci film ini.

In the Country

Weather

Today it is ...
    cloudy
    windy
    warm
    cold
    wet
    raining
What time is ...
    sunrise
    sunset

Hari ini ...
    mendung
    banyak kena angin
    panas
    dingin
    basah
    turun hujan
Berapa jam ...
    matahari terbit
    matahari terbenam

Sights

How far to the ...
    beach
    caves
    forest
    hill
    hot springs
    lake
    mountain
I want to go to the ...
    river
    sea
    volcano
    waterfall

Berapa lama ke ...
    pantai
    gua
    hutan
    bukit
    air panas
    danau
    gunung
Saya mau pergi ke ...
    sungai
    laut
    gunung api
    air terjun

When you go camping or hiking in Indonesia, you will discover that most directions are given in terms of compass points, left and right are not used very often. The compass points are:

north	*utara*
south	*selatan*
east	*timur*
west	*barat*

Indonesians are very polite people and like to be agreeable. If you simply ask 'Is this north?', they will usually just agree with you so it's preferable to use *Dimana utara?* (Where is north?) to get your bearings. Ask several different people if there is any doubt. Remember that in Bali 'north' traditionally means towards the mountains.

Some useful words

ant	*semut*
bird	*burung*
camp (v)	*perkemah*
cat	*kucing*
climb (v)	*naik*
cow	*sapi*
dive (v)	*selam*
dog	*anjing*
fish (v)	*memancing*
fish (n)	*ikan*
flower	*bunga*
frog	*kodok*
horse	*kuda*
hunt (v)	*berburu*
insect	*periksa*

monkey	*kera*
mosquito	*nyamuk*
rope	*tali*
sand	*pasir*
shells	*batok*
sleeping bag	*tas tidur*
snake	*ular*
stone	*batu*
swim (v)	*berenang*
tent	*bemah*
tiger	*harimau*
tool	*alat*
tree	*pohon*
waves	*ombak*

Some useful phrases

How far to the summit?

Berapa lama ke atas?

Please tell me some of the places I should visit.

Tolong sebutkan nama-nama tempat yang harus saya kunjungi.

Is it safe to swim here?

Aman berenang disini?

There are two caves near the hot springs.

Ada dua gua dekat air panas.

Health

Hopefully your time in Indonesia will be without illness and you will not need to turn to this section at all.

Sakit is an all-purpose word about illness. As a verb *sakit* means to feel sick or to hurt, as an adjective it means sick or painful. For example:

the hospital	*rumah sakit*
I feel ill	*Saya sakit.*
My tooth hurts	*Gigi saya sakit.*

Where is the . . .	*Dimana ada . . .*
hospital	*rumah sakit*
pharmacy	*apotik*
drug store	*toko obat*
medicine	*obat-obat*
doctor	*dokter*
dentist	*doktergigi*
I'm sick with . . .	*Saya sakit . . .*
flu	*influenza*
cholera	*kolera*
typhoid	*demam tipus*
malaria	*malaria*
dysentery	*disenteri*
My . . . hurts.	*. . . saya sakit.*
tooth	*gigi*
leg/foot	*kaki*
arm	*lengan*
nose	*hidung*
liver	*hati*

bone	*tulang*
head	*kepala*
stomach	*perut*
I need medicine for . . .	*Saya perlu obat untuk . . .*
lice	*kutu*
headache	*sakit kepala*
stomach ache	*sakit perut*
diarrhoea	*berak berak*
constipation	*sembelit*

Medicine — *Obat-obat*

antibiotics	*antibiotis*
lotion	*cairon*
quinine	*kina*
sleeping pills	*pil tidur*
tablet	*tablet*

Some useful words

allergic	*alergis*
bandage	*pembalut*
bleed (v)	*berdarah*
blood	*darah*
break (v)	*pecah*
breath	*nafas*
burn (n)	*bakar*
careful	*hati-hati*
catch cold	*masuk angin*
collapse (v)	*ambruk*
compress	*kompres*
cough (v)	*batuk*
disease	*penyakit*
fast (v,n)	*puasa*

fever	*demam*
health	*kesehatan*
infection	*infeksi*
itch	*gatal*
injection	*suntik*
pain	*sakit*
poisonous	*beracun*
prescription	*resep*
rheumatism	*encok*
strange	*aneh*
vomit (vb)	*muntah*

Some useful phrases

Please call a taxi.
Tolong panggil taksi.

My leg is broken.
Tolong kaki saya patah.

I need a receipt for my insurance.
Saya perlu kwitansi untuk asuransi saya.

Please take us to a hospital.
Bawa kami ke rumah sakit.

Please buy medicine for me at the pharmacy.
Tolong beli obat untuk saya di apotik.

These tablets must be taken three times a day.
Tablet tablet ini harus diminum tiga kali sehari.

Please shake the bottle before taking.
Hendaklah botolnya dikocok dulu sebelum diminum.

Time

day	*hari*
week	*minggu*
month	*bulan*
year	*tahun*

Days of the week

Monday	*Hari Senen*
Tuesday	*Hari Selasa*
Wednesday	*Hari Rabu*
Thursday	*Hari Kamis*
Friday	*Hari Jumat*
Saturday	*Hari Sabta*
Sunday	*Hari Minggu*

Months

January	*Januari*
February	*Pebruari*
March	*Maret*
April	*April*
May	*Mei*
June	*Juni*
July	*Juli*
August	*Augustus*
September	*September*
October	*Oktober*
November	*Nopember*
December	*Desember*

The number of the day precedes the name of the month in Indonesian dates.

17 August 1945 (Independence Day)
tujuhbelas Augustus sembilanbelas empatbuluh lima

Some useful phrases
What day is it today?
   Hari apa sekarang?
What date is it today?
   Tanggal berapa hari ini?

Telling the time
Some useful words

hour	*jam*
minute	*menit*
second	*dedik*
plus (past)	*liwat*
minus (to)	*kurang*
half	*setengah*

Some useful phrases
What time is it?
   Jam berapa?
It is three o'clock.
   Jam tiga.
It is ten past three.
   Jam tiga liwat sepuluh.
It is ten to four.
   Jam empat kurang sepuluh.
It is rubber time.
   Jam karet (Always gets a laugh)

It is five-thirty.
Jam setengah enam.

Unlike in English, five thirty is not given in Indonesian as half past five but as half to six.

Present time

today	*hari ini*
this week	*minggu ini*
this month	*bulan ini*
this year	*tahun ini*
now	*sekarang*

Past time

yesterday	*kemarin*
last week	*minggu lalu*
last month	*bulan lalu*
last year	*tahun lalu*
ago	*yang lalu*
already	*sudah*
before	*sebelum*
just now	*baru saja*

Future time

tomorrow	*besok*
day after tomorrow	*lusa*
next week	*minggu depan*
next month	*bulan depan*
next year	*tahun depan*
later	*nanti*
after	*sesudah*
not yet	*belum*

Numbers

Indonesian numbers are counted as they are written, from left to right. The numbers from one to ten, then the teens are counted with the suffix *belas*. The numbers after that are counted in multiples of ten – *puluh*. *Sepuluh* is ten, *duapuluh* is twenty and so on until the hundreds, when the suffix *ratus* is used. So *seratus* is one hundred, *duaratus* is two hundred and so on. *Ribu* is thousand, so *seribu* is one thousand, *duaribu* two thousand etc.

0	*nol*	20	*duapuluh*
1	*satu*	21	*duapuluh satu*
2	*dua*	22	*duapuluh dua*
3	*tiga*	23	*duapuluh tiga*
4	*empat*	24	*duapuluh empat*
5	*lima*		
6	*enam*	30	*tigapuluh*
7	*tujuh*	40	*empatpuluh*
8	*delapan*	50	*limapuluh*
9	*sembilan*		
10	*sepuluh*	100	*seratus*
11	*sebelas*	200	*duaratus*
12	*duabelas*	300	*tigaratus*
13	*tigabelas*		
14	*empatbelas*	1000	*seribu*
15	*limabelas*	2000	*duaribu*
16	*enambelas*	3000	*tigaribu*
17	*tujuhbelas*		
18	*delapanbelas*	1,000,000	*sejuta*
19	*sembilanbelas*	2,000,000	*dua juta*

| 268 | *duaratus enampuluh delapan* |
| 51,783 | *limapuluh seribu, tujuhratus delapanpuluh tiga* |

Fractions

1/2	*setengah*
1/4	*seperempat*
3/4	*tiga per empat*

Ordinal numbers

first	*pertama*
second	*kedua*
third	*ketiga*
fourth	*keempat*

Quantity

Some useful words

about	*kira-kira*
enough	*cukup*
few	*sedikit*
many	*banyak*
minus	*kurang*
more	*lagi*
one more	*satu lagi*
number	*nomor*
plus	*tambah*
quantity	*jumlah*
too ...	*terlalu ...*

Vocabulary

A

about – *kira-kira*
above – *diatas*
address – *alamat*
adult – *orang dewasa*
aerogramme – *aerogram*
after – *sesudah*
again – *sekali lagi*
age – *umur*
ago – *yang lalu*
airmail – *pos udara*
airport – *lapangan udara*
all – *semua*
allergic – *allergis*
alley – *gang*
already – *sudah*
also – *juga*
always – *selalu*
animal – *binatang*
ant – *semut*
antibiotics – *antibiotis*
apple – *apel*
arm – *lengan*
arrive – *datang*
artist – *seniman*
ask – *bertanya*
at – *di*

B

bad – *jahat*
baggage – *barang-barang*

ballpoint pen – *pena bolpoin*
banana – *pisang*
bank – *bank*
bank clerk – *pegawai bank*
bank draft – *surat wesel*
barber – *tukang pangkas*
bargain – *tawar*
basket – *tas*
bath – *mandi*
bathe – *mandi*
beach – *pantai*
beans – *buncis*
beautiful – *indah*
because – *karena*
bed – *meja*
beef – *daging sapi*
beer – *bir*
before – *sebelum*
between – *antara*
bicycle – *sepeda*
big – *besar*
bill – *rekening*
bill (money) – *uang kertas*
bird – *turung*
black – *hitam*
blanket – *selimut*
bleed – *berdarah*
blood – *darah*
blue – *biru*
board – *rumah kos*
boat – *prahu*

boil – *merebus*
boiled egg – *telur rebus*
boiled water – *air putih*
bone – *tulang*
book – *buku*
bookshop – *toko buku*
both – *keduanya*
bottle – *botol*
boy – *laki-laki*
brains – *otak*
branch (office) – *cabang*
bread – *roti*
break – *pecah*
breakfast – *makan pagi*
breath – *nafas*
broken – *patah*
brother – *saudara*
brown – *coklat*
burn (n) – *bakar*
bus – *bis*
bus station – *stasiun, terminal bis*
businessman – *pengusaha*
buttons – *kancing*
buy – *beli*

C

cabin – *ruang*
cake – *kue*
camera – *alat pemotret*
camp (v) – *perkemah*
candle – *lilin*
car – *mobil, oto*
careful – *hati-hati*
cash – *uang konton*

cat – *kucing*
cave – *gua*
chair – – *kursi*
cheap – *murah*
cheque – *cek*
chicken – *ayam*
child – *anak*
children – *anak-anak*
chilli – *lombok*
chocolate – *coklat*
cholera – *kolera*
cigarettes – *rokok*
cinema – *bioskop*
city – *kota besar*
clean (adj) – *bersih*
climb (v) – *naik*
closed – *tutup*
clothing – *pakaian*
cloudy – *mendung*
coconut – *kelapa*
coffee – *kopi*
coins – *uang logam*
cold – *dingin*
collapse – *ambruk*
colour – *warna*
comb – *sisir*
come – *datang*
commission – *komisi*
compress – *kompres*
concert – *konser*
confirmation – *penegasan*
constipation – *sembilat*
cook (v) – *masak*
cordial – *es stroop*
corner – *sudut*

cough (v) – *batuk*
cow – *sapi*
crab – *kepiting*
cremation – *pembakaram mayat*
crossroad – *perempatan*
crowded – *ramai*
cucumber – *mentimun*
cup – *cangkir*

D

date – *tanggal*
day – *hari*
day after tomorrow – *lusa*
delicious – *enak*
dentist – *doktergigi*
depart – *berangkat*
deposit – *titip*
develop (film) – *mencuci*
diarrhoea – *berak berak*
dictionary – *kamus*
different – *lain*
difficult – *sukar*
dinner – *makan malam*
dirty – *kotor*
disease – *penyakit*
dive (v) – *selam*
dock – *dok*
doctor – *dokter*
dog – *anjing*
do – *buat*
door – *pintu*
drink – *minum*
drug store – *toko obat*
drunk – *mabuk*

dry – *kering*
duck – *daging bebek*
during – *selama*
dust (n) – *debu*
dysentery – *disenteri*

E

each – *tiap-tiap*
early – *pagi-pagi*
east – *timur*
easy – *mudah*
eat – *makan*
egg – *telur*
electricity – *listrik*
embassy – *kedutaan*
emergency – *darurat*
empty (adj) – *kosong*
endorsement – *pengesyahan*
enough – *cukup*
entrance – *masuk*
envelope – *amplop*
every – *masing-masing*
everybody – *semua orang*
everything – *segala sesuatu*
excuse me – *permisi*
expensive – *mahal*
export (v) – *mengekspor*
eye – *mata*

F

face – *muka*
family – *keluarga*
fan – *kipas*
farmer – *petani*
fast (n, v) – *puasa*

fast (adj) – *cepat*
father – *bapak*
fever – *demam*
few – *sedikit*
film – *film*
finished – *habis*
fish (n) – *ikan*
fish (v) – *memancing*
flower – *bunga*
food – *makanan*
food stall – *warung*
foot – *kaki*
for – *untuk*
foreign – *asing*
foreigner – *orang asing*
forest – *hutan*
fork – *garpu*
fresh – *baru*
friend – *kawan*
frog – *kodok*
from – *dari*
fried – *goreng*
full – *ramai*

G
garden – *kebun*
girl – *perempuan*
give – *memberi*
glass – *gelas*
go – *pergi*
gold – *mas*
good – *bagus*
green – *hijau*

H
half – *setengah*
hammer – *palu*
harbour – *pelabuhan*
hat – *topi*
head – *kepala*
headache – *sakit kepala*
health – *kesehatan*
heart – *jantung*
hedge – *pagar*
here – *disini*
hill – *bukit*
horn – *tanduk*
horse – *kuda*
hospital – *rumah sakit*
hot – *panas*
hotel – *hotel*
hour – *jam*
how – *bagaimana*
how much – *berapa*
hunt (v) – *berburu*
husband – *suami*

I
I – *saya*
identification – *surat keterangan*
if – *kalau*
immediately – *dengan segera*
indigenous – *asli*
infection – *infeksi*
insect – *periksa*
insurance – *assuransi*
interesting – *menarik hati*
intersection – *persimpangan*

itch – *gatal*
ivory – *gading*

J
jar – *toples*
jewellery – *intan permata*
just – *baru*
just one – *satu saja*

K
key – *kunci*
knife – *pisau*
know (v) – *tahu*

L
lake – *danau*
lamb – *domba*
late – *terlambat*
later – *nanti*
leather – *kulit*
left (opp. right) – *kiri*
leg – *kaki*
lemon – *jeruk asam*
letter – *surat*
lice – *kutu*
life – *hidup, hayat*
like (v) – *suka*
little, a – *sedikit*
live (exist/dwell) – *tinggal*
liver – *hati*
lock – *kunci*
long – *panjang*
long (time) – *lama*
look – *lihat*
lotion – *cairon*

lounge – *kamar tinggu*
lunch – *makan siang*

M
make (v) – *membuat*
malaria – *malaria*
man – *orang laki-laki*
mango – *mangga*
many – *banyak*
map – *peta*
market – *pasar*
marital status – *kawin*
mask – *topeng*
matches – *korek*
material – *kain panjang*
may – *boleh*
meat – *daging*
medicine – *obat-obat*
menu – *daftar*
milk – *susu*
minute – *menit*
mirror – *cermin*
money – *uang*
monkey – *kera*
month – *bulan*
more – *lagi*
morning – *pagi*
mosque – *mesjid*
mosquito – *nyamuk*
mosquito net – *kelambu*
most – *paling*
mother – *ibu*
motor cycle – *sepeda motor*
Moslem – *orang Islam*
mountain – *gunung*

much – *banyak*
must – *harus*
museum – *musium*
mutton – *kambing*
Mr – *Bapak*
Mrs – *Nyonya*
Miss – *Nona*

N

name – *nama*
napkin – *serbet*
nationality – *kebangsaan*
near – *dekat*
need – *perlu*
never – *tak pernah*
never mind – *tidak apa-apa*
newspaper – *koran*
nice – *bagus*
night – *malam*
no, not – *tidak*
noisy – *bising*
noodles – *mie*
north – *utara*
nose – *hidung*
not yet – *belum*
now – *sekarang*
number – *nomor*
nurse – *jururawat*

O

occupation – *pekerjaan*
often – *sering*
old – *tua*
older brother – *abang*
older sister – *kakak*

onion – *bawang*
only – *hanya*
open – *buka*
or – *atau*
orange – *jeruk manis*
order (v) – *suruh*
over here – *disini*
over there – *disana*

P

pain – *sakit*
paintings – *lukisan*
papaya – *betik*
paper – *kertas*
parcel – *paket, bungkus*
park – *tamar*
pay (v) – *bayar*
peanuts – *kacang*
pepper – *merika*
perhaps – *barangkali*
person – *orang*
pharmacy – *apotik*
photograph – *foto*
pillow – *bantal*
pineapple – *nanas*
plane – *pesawat terbang*
plate – *piring*
please – *silakan/tolong*
plus – *tambah*
poisonous – *beracun*
police – *polisi*
pork – *daging babi*
port – *kiri kapal*
possibly – *mungkin*
post office – *kantor pos*

postage – *bea*
postcard – *kartu pos*
potato – *kentang*
prefer (v) – *lebih suka*
prescription – *resep*
profession – *pekerjaan*
puppets – *wayang kulit*

Q

quality – *kwalitet*
quantity – *jumlah*
quiet – *tenang*
quinine – *kina*

R

rain – *hujan*
red – *merah*
religion – *agama*
rent (v) – *menyewa*
reservation – *pesenan tempat*
restaurant – *rumah makan*
return – *kembali*
rheumatism – *encok*
rice – *nasi*
right – *kanan*
ring – *cincin*
river – *sungai*
road – *jalan*
roof – *atap*
room – *kamar*
rope – *tampar, tali*
round – *bulat*

S

sail – *layar*

sailor – *pelaut*
salt – *garam*
salty – *asin*
same – *sama-sama*
sand – *pasir*
sandals – *sandel*
school – *sekolah*
sea – *laut*
season – *musim*
seat – *tempat duduk*
seat belt – *sabuk*
second – *dedik*
see – *lihat*
sell – *jual*
send (v) – *kirim*
servant – *pembantu*
service charge – *onkos pelayanan*
shampoo – *keramas*
sheet – *seperai*
shells – *batok*
ship – *kapal*
shrimp – *udang*
shoe laces – *tali spatu*
shop – *toko*
signature – *tandatangan*
silver – *perak*
since – *sejak*
singer – *penyani*
sister – *saudara*
sit – *duduk*
sleep (v) – *tidur*
sleeping bag – *tas tidur*
slice (v) – *iris*
slow – *pelan*

small – *kecil*
snake – *ular*
soap – *sabun*
some – *lain*
sorry – *ma'af*
sour – *asam*
south – *selatan*
soy sauce – *kecap asin*
spicy – *pedas*
spoon – *sendok*
stamps – *meterai pos*
stationmaster – *kepala stasiun*
stomach – *perut*
stomache ache – *sakit perut*
stone – *batu*
stop (v) – *berhenti*
strange – *aneh*
street – *jalan*
style – *macam*
suitcase – *kopor*
surface mail – *pos biasa*
sweet (adj) – *manis*
sweets – *gula-gula*
swim (v) – *berenang*
swimsuit – *pakaian mandi*

T
table – *meja*
tablet – *tablet*
tailor – *penjahit*
take off – *barangkat*
tampons – *tampon*
tax – *pajak*
taxi – *taksi*
tea – *teh*

teacher – *guru*
telegram – *kawat*
telephone – *telepon*
teller – *kasir*
temple – *kuil*
tent – *bemah*
thank you – *terima kasih*
that – *itu*
there is – *ada*
they – *mereka*
theatre – *gedung sandiwara*
thirsty – *haus*
this – *ini*
thread – *benang*
ticket – *karcis*
ticket window – *loket*
tiger – *harimau*
timetable – *daftar*
to – *ke*
today – *hari ini*
toilet – *kamar kecil*
toilet paper – *kertas kamar kecil*
tomorrow – *besok*
too – *terlalu*
tool – *alat*
tooth – *gigi*
toothbrush – *sikatgigi*
torch – *obor*
towel – *handuk*
train – *kereta api*
travellers' cheque – *cek turis*
tree – *pohon*
truck – *prahoto*
typhoid – *demam tipus*

U

understand (v) – *mengerti*
underwear – *pakaian dalam*
unripe – *mentah*

V

very – *sangat*
village – *desa*
volcano – *gunung api*
vomit – *muntah*

W

wake – *bangun*
walk – *jalan kaki*
want (v) – *mau*
warm – *panas*
wash – *cuci*
water – *air*
waterfall – *air terjun*
waves – *ombak*
we – *kami, kita*
week – *minggu*
west – *barat*
wet – *basah*
what – *apa*

when – *bila*
where – *dimana*
which – *yang mana*
white – *putih*
who – *siapa*
why – *mengapa*
wife – *isteri*
window – *jendela*
with – *dengan*
without – *tanpa*
woman – *perempuan*
wood (timber) – *kayu*
woodcarving – *ukiran kayu*
writer – *penulis*
writing paper – *kertas kulis*

Y

yellow – *kuning*
yes – *ya*
yesterday – *kemarin*
you – *saudara*

Z

zoo – *kebun binatang*